About the Author

With a distinguished military career in Communications and IT, the author brings a wealth of experience and a unique perspective to the field of cybersecurity. Leveraging over two decades of expertise in digital security, they have successfully transitioned from military service to private industry, positioning themselves as a credible voice in quantum cryptography. Their dedication to safeguarding organizations against evolving digital threats underscores their passion for this critical field, making complex topics accessible and engaging for a diverse audience.

Throughout their career, the author has worked with both local and central government departments in the UK, developing and implementing robust security measures to combat a range of threats. Their military discipline combined with rich industry experience equips them with exceptional insights into the ever-evolving landscape of cybersecurity. As a veteran of the UK Armed Forces, they approach challenges with a strategic mindset, ensuring that organizations are not only prepared but resilient against potential cyber risks.

The author's educational pursuits have significantly influenced their writing and professional journey. With a strong foundation in technology and information systems, their academic background complements their practical experience in the field. Inspired by the urgent need for greater awareness and understanding of cybersecurity issues, they began writing to share their knowledge and practical insights. This book, "Cyber Security Quantum Cryptography," emerges from their desire to demystify complex concepts and empower organizations and individuals alike to prioritize their digital safety.

What sets the author apart is their genuine passion for making cybersecurity relatable and engaging. They believe in a hands-on approach, using real-world experiences to illustrate key points, and strive to foster an atmosphere of curiosity and learning among their readers. By breaking down intricate topics into digestible segments, they cultivate a deeper understanding of the subject matter, encouraging proactive engagement in the implementation of effective security measures.

As a committed advocate for cybersecurity education, the author aims to inspire a new generation of professionals to take on this critical challenge. Their mission is not only to inform but also to empower readers to recognize the importance of cyber resilience in today's digital age. Looking ahead, they aspire to contribute further to the field through speaking engagements, consulting, and continued writing, ensuring that cybersecurity remains a priority in an increasingly complex world.

Table of Contents

Chapter 1: Introduction to Quantum Cryptography

Chapter 2: Fundamentals of Quantum Mechanics

Chapter 3: Key Concepts in Cryptography

Chapter 4: Quantum Key Distribution (QKD)

Chapter 5: Practical Implementations of Quantum Cryptography

(1) - 5.1 Laboratory Setups for QKD

(2) - 5.2 Commercial Applications of Quantum Cryptography

(3) - 5.3 Scaling Quantum Cryptography Solutions

Chapter 6: Security Analysis of Quantum Cryptography

Chapter 7: Comparing Quantum and Classical Cryptography

Chapter 8: Quantum Cryptography in the Enterprise

(1) - 8.1 Assessing Organizational Readiness

(2) - 8.2 Integrating Quantum Solutions into Existing Systems

(3) - 8.3 Training and Development for Security Teams

Chapter 9: Policy and Regulatory Considerations

(1) - 9.1 International Standards for Quantum Cryptography

(2) - 9.2 Compliance and Legal Implications

(3) - 9.3 Ethical Considerations in Data Protection

Chapter 10: Challenges in Quantum Cryptography Deployment

Chapter 11: Future Trends in Quantum Cryptography

Chapter 12: Real-World Case Studies

Chapter 13: Quantum Computers and Their Impact on Cyber Security

Chapter 14: Collaboration and Research in Quantum Cryptography

Chapter 15: Conclusion and Final Thoughts

Chapter 1: Introduction to Quantum Cryptography

1.1 The Evolution of Cryptography

The history of cryptography is a fascinating journey that traces the evolution of secret communication from ancient times to the cutting-edge technologies of today. Early cryptographic methods emerged with simple techniques such as substitution ciphers, a concept seen in the Caesar cipher used by Julius Caesar to protect his military messages. As civilizations advanced, so did their cryptographic methods. The Middle Ages witnessed the use of the polyalphabetic cipher, which introduced complexity by utilizing multiple alphabets to encode messages, thus providing more security against cryptanalysis. The invention of the telegraph and the subsequent development of mechanical encrypting devices in the 19th century marked significant milestones, leading to innovations like the one-time pad and the Enigma machine during World War II, which played crucial roles in military communications. However, the digital age brought about a new paradigm, shifting from classical approaches to modern, algorithm-based methods. The advent of public-key cryptography in the 1970s, introduced by Whitfield Diffie and Martin Hellman, revolutionized how secure communication could be established over unsecured channels, enabling the widespread use of the internet and electronic communications.

The transition to quantum cryptography represents the next major leap in this evolutionary process. Quantum Key Distribution (QKD) leverages the principles of quantum mechanics to create a theoretically unbreakable encryption method. By using quantum bits, or qubits, which exist in multiple states simultaneously, QKD can detect any eavesdropping attempts during the key exchange process. This groundbreaking technology has the potential to bolster digital security against the rising threat of quantum computers, which possess the capability to crack traditional encryption methods through brute force attacks. As researchers continue to explore quantum algorithms and protocols, the cybersecurity landscape is poised for a significant transformation that offers unprecedented protection against cyber threats.

Throughout its long history, cryptography has seen major milestones that have shaped its development and implications for digital security. The introduction of the RSA algorithm in 1977 is one such landmark achievement that established a new standard for secure communication on the internet. RSA cryptography relies on the mathematical properties of large prime numbers, making it exceedingly difficult to crack without the correct key. In the late 1990s and early 2000s, the shift to more secure algorithms like AES (Advanced Encryption Standard) further solidified cryptographic practices in both governmental and commercial sectors. As the stakes for digital security continue to rise, the implications of these advancements become ever more critical. Each innovation not only enhanced our ability to safeguard information but also laid the groundwork for emerging solutions like post-quantum cryptography, which aims to create new standards secure against quantum threats. Understanding these milestones equips cybersecurity professionals with the necessary insights to anticipate future challenges and adapt their strategies for effective defense against sophisticated cyber adversaries.

Keeping abreast of advancements in cryptography is essential for cybersecurity professionals. The rapid evolution of technology necessitates an ongoing commitment to learning and adaptation. Investing time in understanding quantum cryptography and its potential impact on future security protocols ensures readiness for tomorrow's challenges. Engaging with academic research, participating in industry forums, or enrolling in specialized training can offer invaluable insights and prepare professionals to face the ongoing transformation of the cybersecurity landscape.

1.2 Principles of Quantum Mechanics

Quantum mechanics introduces transformative concepts that are pivotal to advancements in cryptographic applications. One of the foremost principles is superposition, which allows quantum bits or qubits to exist in multiple states simultaneously. This property exponentially increases the computational power available for processing complex algorithms. When combined with another essential feature, entanglement, systems of qubits can become interlinked in such a way that the state of one qubit directly influences the state of another, regardless of the distance separating them. This characteristic has profound implications for the security of data transmission. In quantum cryptography, these principles can be harnessed to develop protocols that ensure secure communication channels, where any attempt at eavesdropping can be detected due to the change in state caused by an observer's measurement.

The intersection of quantum mechanics and information theory creates a new framework for understanding data security. Classical information theory relies on principles that assume the existence of bits capable of being either 0 or 1, leading to conventional cryptographic measures that often rely on computational difficulty to secure data. However, quantum information theory alters this landscape. By applying quantum principles such as superposition and entanglement, information no longer has to reside in a binary framework. Instead, it can exist in a more complex multidimensional space. This opens doors for quantum key distribution (QKD), which leverages these quantum states to generate cryptographic keys with a level of security unattainable by classical methods. The ability to detect any intruder through disturbances in the qubit state ensures that quantum cryptographic techniques represent the future of robust cybersecurity practices.

As the cybersecurity landscape evolves, understanding these quantum principles becomes essential for professionals looking to enhance security protocols against the advancing capabilities of quantum computing. Integrating quantum mechanics with information theory isn't just an academic exercise; it is a vital step toward developing encryption methods that can withstand the challenges posed by future technologies. Keeping abreast of developments in quantum cryptography and actively participating in discussions and research on this front can greatly benefit cybersecurity efforts aimed at maintaining the integrity and confidentiality of sensitive information.

1.3 The Need for Quantum Cryptography

Classical cryptography has long served as the backbone of secure communications in our digital world. However, the advance of quantum computing brings formidable vulnerabilities that could render many existing cryptographic methods obsolete. Notably, algorithms like RSA and ECC rely on the computational difficulty of problems such as integer factorization and discrete logarithms. Quantum computers, powered by qubits, utilize principles of superposition and entanglement to solve these problems exponentially faster than classical computers. Consequently, what would take today's supercomputers thousands of years to crack, a sufficiently powerful quantum computer could achieve in mere minutes. This chilling possibility creates an urgent need for discussions among cyber security professionals regarding the limitations of classical cryptography and the imperative to transition to quantum-resistant systems.

As awareness of these vulnerabilities grows, so does the necessity for quantum solutions to safeguard sensitive data. Quantum cryptography offers a revolutionary approach to securing information through principles like quantum key distribution (QKD), which guarantees the confidentiality of exchanged keys. Unlike traditional methods that can be intercepted without detection, QKD leverages the fundamental tenets of quantum mechanics, ensuring that any attempt to eavesdrop alters the quantum state, alerting the parties involved. This provides a robust framework capable of protecting data against future threats posed by quantum computing. By embracing quantum solutions, cyber security professionals can establish a new standard for encryption that promises resilience against potential breaches, safeguarding vital information in an era of unprecedented technological advancement. The transition may require significant investment and effort, yet the protection of sensitive data demands this proactive approach to future-proofing security measures.

Staying abreast of developments in quantum cryptography is critical for cyber security professionals. Engaging in ongoing education and integrating quantum technologies into existing infrastructures will become increasingly important as quantum threats materialize. Consider participating in industry workshops or collaborating with research institutions focused on quantum technologies. Developing a mindset open to adopting these advanced solutions will equip professionals to not only address current vulnerabilities but also to defend against the ever-evolving landscape of cyber threats.

Chapter 2: Fundamentals of Quantum Mechanics

2.1 Quantum States and Superposition

Quantum states represent the fundamental properties of quantum systems. In essence, a quantum state encapsulates everything that can be known about a particle, such as its position, momentum, and spin. The principle of superposition is a key feature of quantum mechanics, allowing a quantum system to exist in multiple states at once until a measurement is performed. This can be illustrated through the famous thought experiment known as Schrödinger's cat, where a cat in a box can be simultaneously alive and dead until someone opens the box to observe its state. Practical examples include quantum bits, or qubits, which can represent both 0 and 1 at the same time, enabling the unique capabilities of quantum computing.

The implications of superposition are significant, especially in the fields of computation and cryptography. In computational contexts, superposition allows quantum computers to process a vast amount of information simultaneously, exponentially speeding up problem-solving capabilities for tasks like factoring large numbers or simulating complex systems. In the realm of cryptography, superposition leads to quantum key distribution (QKD) methods that promise unprecedented security. Utilizing the principles of superposition and entanglement, QKD can ensure that any attempt to eavesdrop on the communication alters the states being transmitted, thereby revealing the presence of an intruder. This creates a foundation for secure communications that are theoretically impervious to hacking efforts traditional encryption methods cannot fully guarantee.

Cybersecurity professionals looking to the future of quantum cryptography should consider the transition to quantum-safe algorithms in their strategies. As the advent of powerful quantum computers approaches, existing encryption methods may become vulnerable. Proactively adopting quantum-resistant cryptographic protocols can help secure sensitive information against evolving threats. Remaining informed about advancements in quantum technology and engaging in discussions surrounding its applications will enable cybersecurity experts to better prepare for the transformations that lie ahead.

2.2 Entanglement and Its Implications

Quantum entanglement is a phenomenon where two or more particles become interconnected in such a way that the state of one particle directly influences the state of another, regardless of the distance separating them. This unique characteristic of quantum mechanics poses fascinating prospects for enhancing security protocols. In the realm of cyber security, entanglement plays a crucial role in creating secure keys for encryption. When two particles are entangled, measuring the state of one immediately provides information about the state of the other. This feature enables the generation of cryptographic keys that are theoretically immune to eavesdropping. If an unauthorized party attempts to intercept or measure the entangled particles, the entanglement is disrupted, alerting the communicating parties of a potential security breach. Hence, incorporating quantum entanglement into security frameworks can significantly bolster data protection strategies.

The potential applications of quantum entanglement in secure communications are vast and transformative. One notable application is quantum key distribution (QKD), which ensures that any attempt to eavesdrop on the communication will be detected. In QKD, two parties can securely share keys using entangled particle pairs, enhancing not only the confidentiality of their communication but also ensuring the integrity of the transmitted information. Additionally, entanglement can contribute to developing faster and more efficient networks through quantum repeaters, which could be vital for long-distance secure communication without the loss of data integrity. As cyber threats evolve, the shift towards entanglement-based communication security becomes even more critical. Therefore, understanding and leveraging quantum entanglement can lead to a more secure future in cyber security, pushing the boundaries of what traditional encryption methods can achieve.

As cyber security professionals look to the future of encryption and communication, it is essential to stay informed about advancements in quantum cryptography. Engaging with the latest research on entanglement and its practical applications can provide valuable insights ranging from theory to implementation. Exploring partnerships with research institutions or investing in quantum computing resources could be advantageous as the technology matures. Keeping abreast of developments in quantum protocols will not only enhance security measures but also position organizations ahead in the competitive landscape of cyber security.

2.3 Measurement in Quantum Mechanics

Measurement in quantum systems is a process that fundamentally alters the state of the system being observed. In classical physics, measurement can be seen as merely a way to gain information about a system without affecting it significantly. However, in quantum mechanics, the act of measuring a quantum system, such as a particle's position or momentum, causes a collapse of the wave function, effectively reducing the range of possible outcomes to a single observed value. This phenomenon reveals a profound principle: the information we glean from quantum systems is intertwined with their unpredictability and can change the state of the system itself. The implications of this behaviour extend far beyond physics and into the realm of information theory, where the very act of observation not only retrieves information but also alters it. As cyber security professionals navigate the complexities of quantum computing and cryptography, understanding this aspect of measurement is crucial because it presents both challenges and opportunities in the field of data protection.

Measurement challenges many traditional assumptions in cryptography, particularly those that rely on the complexity of mathematical problems as the basis for security. Classical cryptographic systems often hinge on the difficulty of tasks such as factoring large numbers or solving discrete logarithm problems. However, the potential of quantum computing raises questions about the efficacy of these methods. Quantum measurement, as we understand, does not just reveal information, it also introduces the possibility of eavesdropping—an observer could theoretically gain knowledge about a quantum system without altering its state in the same way a classical measurement would. This creates new vulnerabilities in cryptographic systems that are predicated on the assumption that observing a cipher does not compromise its integrity. As such, quantum cryptography offers a promising alternative by leveraging the principles of quantum mechanics to create secure communication channels that can detect eavesdroppers. Cyber security professionals must adapt their understanding of both measurement and the nature of information flows to implement systems that remain secure against the evolving threats posed by quantum technologies.

Staying ahead in the realm of cyber security means embracing these new insights from quantum mechanics. It's imperative to explore quantum key distribution, which guarantees the security of keys through quantum states, and be prepared to update classical encryption methods in anticipation of future quantum developments. Developing an understanding of how quantum measurement can be harnessed for secure communication will be crucial as we transition into an era where quantum capabilities become more prevalent. By focusing on integrating quantum-safe solutions into current infrastructures, cyber security professionals can ensure a robust defense strategy against both current and future threats.

Chapter 3: Key Concepts in Cryptography

3.1 Classical Cryptographic Techniques

Classical cryptographic techniques form the bedrock of modern cryptography, providing essential methods for secure communication. Among these, symmetric and asymmetric encryption play pivotal roles. Symmetric encryption relies on a single key that both encrypts and decrypts the data. Examples include algorithms like the Data Encryption Standard (DES) and the Advanced Encryption Standard (AES). These methods are efficient and well-suited for encrypting large amounts of data due to their speed. However, the challenge lies in secure key distribution; both parties must exchange the key securely without interception. In contrast, asymmetric encryption uses a pair of keys: a public key for encryption and a private key for decryption. This technique underpins protocols like RSA, allowing secure communication without the need for both parties to share a secret key beforehand. Asymmetric methods are crucial in establishing secure channels over insecure networks, such as the internet, particularly in transactions and authentication processes.

Evaluating the effectiveness of these classical techniques in the context of contemporary security challenges reveals both their strengths and limitations. While symmetric encryption remains robust against conventional attacks, advancements in computing power and techniques such as brute-force attacks pose significant risks. As a response, modern implementations often utilize larger key sizes to enhance security. Asymmetric encryption, too, is effective but vulnerable to specific quantum attacks, such as those proposed by Shor's algorithm, which could factor large numbers exponentially faster than classical algorithms. Consequently, the applicability of classical methods is now being scrutinized in the light of quantum computing, which threatens to undermine their foundational security assumptions. Cybersecurity professionals must recognize that while these classical techniques continue to serve valuable purposes today, they should also be aware of the necessity to evolve towards quantum-resistant algorithms to safeguard future communications.

In the competitive landscape of cybersecurity, understanding classical techniques is crucial but preparing for the future is paramount. Professionals should familiarize themselves with emerging quantum cryptographic methods, which aim to harness the principles of quantum mechanics to create fundamentally secure communication channels. Engaging in discussions about post-quantum cryptography will enable security experts to stay ahead of potential threats and ensure that the measures in place can withstand next-generation attacks. Regularly updating skills and knowledge about both classical and quantum cryptographic techniques will provide a solid foundation for safeguarding sensitive information in an ever-evolving digital world.

3.2 Security Protocols and Algorithms

In today's cybersecurity landscape, several protocols and algorithms have gained prominence due to their effectiveness in safeguarding digital information. Protocols like SSL/TLS, which secure communications over the internet, have become foundational for safe e-commerce and online transactions. They employ encryption methods to protect data in transit, ensuring that sensitive information remains confidential and intact. Similarly, IPsec is widely used to secure Internet Protocol communications by authenticating and encrypting each IP packet, making it crucial for VPN technology. On the cryptographic front, algorithms such as AES, RSA, and ECC have been instrumental in providing secure encryption, authentication, and integrity checks. AES is particularly favoured for its speed and security in encrypting vast amounts of data, while RSA and ECC offer robust asymmetric encryption methods that are central to key exchange and digital signatures. The choice of these protocols and algorithms underscores a commitment to robust security measures amidst increasing threats.

As quantum computing evolves, the threat it poses to traditional cryptographic methods cannot be overstated. Quantum computers leverage principles of quantum mechanics to solve complex problems at speeds unattainable by classical computers. This capability jeopardizes widely used algorithms like RSA and ECC, which rely on the difficulty of factoring large numbers or solving discrete logarithm problems. Quantum threats necessitate a re-evaluation of the security protocols currently in use. Initiatives like the Quantum Internet aim to develop protocols inherently resistant to quantum attacks by utilizing quantum key distribution (QKD). This QKD utilizes the principles of quantum mechanics to secure communication channels against interception. As we advance, it becomes crucial for cybersecurity professionals to not only stay informed about existing protocols but also to adapt to the forthcoming changes in cryptography driven by quantum technologies. It is advisable to invest time in understanding quantum-resistant algorithms and engage with ongoing discussions and research in post-quantum cryptography. Being proactive in this space will significantly strengthen defenses against the inevitable challenges posed by quantum advancements.

3.3 Limitations of Classical Cryptography

Classical cryptography, while a vital part of historical security frameworks, reveals inherent weaknesses when scrutinized under the lens of modern cyber threats. One of the significant shortcomings is its susceptibility to various forms of cryptanalysis. Traditional algorithms, such as Caesar and Vigenère ciphers, rely heavily on the secrecy of their keys and the assumption that potential attackers lack sufficient resources or knowledge to decode the messages. However, with advancements in computational capabilities and the prevalence of sophisticated tools, these assumptions no longer hold true. Attackers can now employ brute force methods or conduct frequency analysis with ease, rendering many classical systems ineffective. Moreover, messages encrypted with classical techniques may also fall prey to interception, where unauthorized parties could capture the keys or plaintexts under certain conditions, further compromising the data's confidentiality and integrity.

To address these limitations, there is a crucial necessity for evolving cryptographic standards that not only meet contemporary security needs but are also resilient against future threats. Traditional methods are giving way to more complex algorithms designed to withstand both classical and quantum attacks. The emergence of post-quantum cryptography aims to develop encryption techniques that are secure against the potential capabilities of quantum computing. These emerging standards utilize mathematical problems that are currently difficult to solve, thus securing data in a way that traditional methods cannot. Cybersecurity professionals must advocate for the adoption of these modern cryptographic protocols, ensuring that organizations remain steps ahead of evolving threats. It is equally important for security policies and practices to be regularly updated, fostering an environment where security is treated as a dynamic challenge rather than a static object that can be solved once and for all. As part of this evolution, ongoing research and testing in quantum cryptography may provide a pathway to achieving truly secure communications, opening doors to possibilities previously thought unattainable.

Chapter 4: Quantum Key Distribution (QKD)

4.1 Overview of QKD Protocols

Quantum Key Distribution (QKD) represents a significant advancement in secure communication, leveraging the principles of quantum mechanics to create cryptographic keys that are fundamentally more secure than those derived from classical methods. Existing protocols include BB84, which uses the polarization of photons to encode information, and E91, which relies on entangled particles. Other notable protocols are the continuous-variable QKD, which utilizes Gaussian-modulated coherent states, and the device-independent QKD that provides security without reliance on the trustworthiness of the equipment used. These protocols not only enable key generation over distances that were previously challenging but also offer mechanisms for error correction and privacy amplification, enhancing overall security against potential eavesdropping attempts. As technology progresses, hybrid protocols that combine classical and quantum systems are emerging, making QKD more versatile and adaptable to existing infrastructures.

The security guarantees offered by QKD distinguish it from classical key distribution methods, mainly through its reliance on the laws of quantum physics rather than computational assumptions. In classical systems, security often depends on the difficulty of mathematical problems, such as factoring large numbers. However, with QKD, any attempt to eavesdrop on the key generation process can be detected due to the inherent property of quantum states being altered upon measurement. This allows parties to verify the integrity of the keys being exchanged. Additionally, the security analysis of QKD protocols can be mathematically proven under the quantum framework, providing a level of assurance that cannot be achieved with purely classical frameworks. Thus, QKD creates a unique and powerful tool in the arsenal of cyber security professionals, offering the promise of truly secure communication.

As cyber security professionals navigate the complexities of modern threats, understanding and integrating QKD technology into future systems can offer a pioneering edge. Being at the forefront of research in quantum cryptography can lead not only to enhanced security for sensitive data but also to a proactive stance against the evolving landscape of cyber attacks. Exploring partnerships with quantum technology firms and investing in training for the workforce in quantum principles will ensure organizations are well-equipped to embrace this transformative technology.

4.2 BB84 Protocol Explained

The BB84 protocol, introduced by Charles Bennett and Gilles Brassard in 1984, is one of the first and most well-known quantum key distribution (QKD) protocols. Its fundamental purpose is to allow two parties to securely exchange encryption keys over a potentially insecure channel. The protocol relies on the principles of quantum mechanics, particularly the behaviour of photons being used to carry information. In BB84, each party (traditionally referred to as Alice and Bob) prepares quantum bits (qubits) which can be in one of two states: either being polarized vertically or horizontally, or diagonally (±45 degrees). The communication occurs in a series of rounds, where Alice sends qubits to Bob in a random fashion and both parties later compare their choices about basis states over a classical channel. This seemingly simple method significantly enhances security because any eavesdropping attempt will disturb the quantum states, alerting both Alice and Bob to the presence of an intruder.

The real-world implications of the BB84 protocol extend beyond theoretical foundations into practical applications in secure communications. Its deployment has been witnessed across various sectors, including financial institutions, government agencies, and telecommunication companies. Notably, a quantum-secured network using BB84 has been established in cities like Zurich and Beijing, where its efficacy in face of eavesdropping attempts has been tested and proven. Such networks are vital as they lay the groundwork for post-quantum cryptography, especially as quantum computing technology evolves. Many organizations are now investing in infrastructures that can support QKD protocols like BB84 as a proactive measure against future quantum attacks. Furthermore, the ongoing research is focused on improving the implementation of BB84 to enable longer distances and higher key rates, making it more accessible for widespread commercial use.

As the landscape of cybersecurity continues to evolve with advancements in quantum computing, professionals in the field should stay informed about quantum-safe security measures. Understanding the principles behind protocols like BB84 and their implementations can provide a significant advantage in future-proofing security practices. Adopting these measures not only secures current communications but also prepares infrastructures for the inevitable integration of quantum technologies, ensuring resilience against emerging threats in the digital world.

4.3 Device-Independent QKD

Device-independent quantum key distribution (QKD) represents a transformative approach in the realm of quantum cryptography, focused on secure communication without relying on specific characteristics of the devices used for the transmission of quantum states. The primary advantage of this paradigm lies in its ability to ensure security even when the devices involved are untrusted or potentially compromised. Traditional QKD protocols often assume that the quantum hardware operates reliably and accurately, but device-independent QKD mitigates these assumptions by using statistical methods to infer what is happening, therefore providing security assurances based solely on the measurement outcomes. This means that even if an adversary has access to the devices, the final key can still be established securely, as long as the overall framework exhibits certain quantum mechanical properties. Such security not only enhances trust among users but also lays the groundwork for broader applications in various sectors where high levels of data protection are paramount.

Despite its promises, the practical implementation of device-independent QKD is fraught with technological requirements and challenges. First and foremost, there is a need for sophisticated quantum technologies that can produce and measure quantum states with high fidelity. These technologies must operate under conditions that minimize noise and loss, which pose significant obstacles, especially over long distances. Furthermore, sophisticated statistical analysis tools are necessary to interpret the measurement data effectively, as the security proofs hinge on these results. The frontiers of quantum communication also require an update to existing networking infrastructures to support the unique needs of quantum keys. Other challenges include ensuring that the quantum channels are optimized for speed and reliability, and that the overall system can scale to meet the demands of real-world applications. Cyber security professionals must be prepared to tackle these challenges head-on, as they represent both barriers and opportunities for the future of secure communications.

Staying conversational with these advancements in mind is vital for cyber security professionals. Embracing continuous education on emerging quantum technologies and understanding their implications can provide a competitive edge. Additionally, investing in partnerships with organizations at the forefront of quantum cryptography can facilitate the adoption of these revolutionary methods, pushing the boundaries of what is possible in terms of secure communication. It is this proactive approach that will enable professionals to navigate the complexities of device-independent QKD and harness its potential for truly secure cyber environments.

Chapter 5: Practical Implementations of Quantum Cryptography

5.1 Laboratory Setups for QKD

Various laboratory setups are essential for conducting Quantum Key Distribution (QKD) experiments effectively. These setups typically involve multiple components, including single-photon sources, beam splitters, detectors, and classical communication channels. One common configuration utilizes a fibre optic system where photons are transmitted over long distances, allowing researchers to study the effects of noise and attenuation on quantum signals. For instance, setups may incorporate polarization encoding techniques to represent bits, where the polarization state of each photon securely carries the key information. The choice of the optical components is crucial because they directly impact the fidelity and security of the QKD process.

Moreover, free-space optical communication setups are also employed, typically in laboratories with specific equipment to mitigate atmospheric disturbances. The use of telescopes and specialized optics enhances the transmission efficiency and facilitates experiments over larger distances without the limitations imposed by fibre optics. In both setups, maintaining the quantum state of the photons throughout the transmission process is a fundamental challenge that researchers constantly strive to overcome. These laboratory environments also often include advanced technologies, like entangled photon pairs, which allow for more sophisticated QKD protocols, enhancing the potential for future applications in secure communications.

Testing QKD systems brings to light various challenges that must be addressed to ensure robustness and reliability. One significant issue faced during experimentation is the potential influence of eavesdroppers. To simulate possible interception, researchers employ various methodologies such as the use of man-in-the-middle scenarios to test the resilience of the QKD protocols in place. Additionally, characterizing the performance of QKD systems necessitates rigorous analysis, including measuring key rates and quantum bit error rates under different environmental conditions. Overcoming technical barriers such as detector efficiency and the integration of QKD systems with existing communication infrastructures requires creative problem-solving and a deep understanding of both quantum mechanics and cyber security principles. Adopting these rigorous testing methodologies is critical, as they enhance the understanding of QKD system vulnerabilities and inform future innovations that will make quantum cryptography a practical solution for securing communications in an increasingly digital world.

Each experiment offers insights that contribute to the advancement of QKD technologies and their potential applications, making it crucial for cyber security professionals to stay updated on these developments. Regularly evaluating the results of laboratory experiments and adapting methodologies will ensure the progression of quantum key distribution in the ever-evolving landscape of cybersecurity.

5.2 Commercial Applications of Quantum Cryptography

Quantum cryptography has begun to find its place in various industries, transforming how organizations handle sensitive information. The financial sector is at the forefront, utilizing quantum key distribution (QKD) to secure transactions and protect client data. Major banks and financial institutions are investing heavily in this technology to thwart cyber threats, enabling them to maintain trust and protect billions of dollars in assets. Additionally, healthcare and biomedical sectors are starting to employ quantum cryptographic techniques to secure patient data and medical records against increasing cyber attacks, thus ensuring compliance with privacy regulations.

Telecommunications companies utilize quantum cryptography to elevate their security measures. By establishing quantum-based secure communication channels, they can prevent interception and eavesdropping on sensitive communications. Noteworthy case studies illustrate the commercialization of quantum cryptography in real-world scenarios. For instance, the Chinese government successfully implemented a nationwide secure communication network using quantum cryptography, showcasing a practical application that protects government communications from potential threats. In the corporate space, a technology firm deployed QKD to protect its intellectual property during product development, effectively shielding trade secrets against industrial espionage.

Enterprises looking to the future must assess their security frameworks with an eye towards integrating quantum cryptography. While the technology is still evolving, adopting its principles can provide a significant competitive edge in terms of data protection. For cybersecurity professionals, staying informed about advancements in quantum cryptography, along with the associated risks and benefits, is vital for designing robust security architectures that can withstand future challenges.

5.3 Scaling Quantum Cryptography Solutions

To scale quantum key distribution (QKD) solutions, understanding the technological and infrastructural requirements is critical. The implementation of QKD demands sophisticated technology to facilitate the generation and distribution of cryptographic keys through quantum channels. This involves the integration of compatible hardware such as single-photon detectors and quantum repeaters, enabling secure data transmission over long distances. It is essential to develop a robust infrastructure, including reliable fibre optic networks and communication satellites, to support the requirements of QKD, especially when considering the physical limitations associated with quantum communication, such as signal loss and environmental disturbances. Moreover, effective error correction protocols must also be in place to ensure the integrity of the keys generated and to maintain the security of transmitted data in real-world conditions.

Market readiness for QKD is another significant factor that impacts broader adoption. As organizations increasingly recognize the susceptibility of traditional encryption methods to quantum computing threats, the urgency for adopting quantum-safe solutions grows. The path to implementation hinges not only on the advancement of QKD technology but also on the establishment of standards, interoperability, and regulatory frameworks. Encouraging collaborations between academia, industry, and government entities will play a vital role in accelerating the deployment of these systems. Training programs for cybersecurity professionals will also be necessary to ensure that the workforce is equipped to manage and operate quantum cryptographic systems effectively.

Building public confidence through awareness and education is equally essential in this transformative landscape. Practical demonstrations of QKD in real-world environments can help illustrate its benefits, thereby fostering broader acceptance among end-users. Fostering partnerships between tech innovators and cybersecurity experts will also lead to development breakthroughs, addressing both the scalability challenges and market readiness. Cybersecurity professionals should focus on these evolving dynamics to leverage the enormous potential of quantum cryptography for enhanced security in the digital realm.

Chapter 6: Security Analysis of Quantum Cryptography

6.1 Threat Models in Quantum Cryptography

Quantum cryptography faces unique challenges, leading to the development of specific threat models tailored to its applications. These models aim to understand potential vulnerabilities and the nature of attacks on quantum key distribution (QKD) systems. One prominent threat model revolves around eavesdropping, where an adversary, often referred to as Eve, attempts to intercept quantum keys while they are being exchanged. The principles of quantum mechanics dictate that any measurement performed on a quantum state inevitably alters that state, thereby revealing the presence of an eavesdropper. Nevertheless, sophisticated strategies, such as collective or individual attacks, can be implemented by an adversary who possesses advanced knowledge and capabilities. Additionally, there is the risk of side-channel attacks, where information is leaked through unintended channels like electromagnetic emissions or even thermal radiation. Such attacks can offer valuable insights regardless of the quantum system's inherent security features.

Analyzing the strengths and weaknesses of these threat models reveals their applicability and limitations. One significant strength is that the unique characteristics of quantum systems provide inherent safeguards against eavesdropping. The laws of quantum mechanics impose a constraint that makes undetected interception virtually impossible under ideal conditions, thereby ensuring a high level of security. However, weaknesses do surface when considering practical implementations and real-world conditions. For instance, hardware vulnerabilities, such as those arising from imperfect detectors or signal amplifiers, can give attackers potential footholds. Moreover, threat models must account for the capabilities of potential adversaries, which continuously evolve, paralleling advancements in technology. As quantum computing develops, the risk landscape will inevitably shift, necessitating an ongoing examination and adaptation of threat models to mitigate emerging risks. Cyber security professionals must remain vigilant and proactive, integrating real-time threat intelligence to ensure robust defenses against evolving threats.

Understanding these threat models in the context of quantum cryptography is not merely an academic exercise; it serves as a critical aspect for security professionals. With the ever-shifting landscape of technology, being aware of the potential risks and the mechanisms of attack can help professionals implement countermeasures effectively. Developing resilience requires an approach that combines quantum-resistant algorithms with continuous monitoring of systems for anomalies or breaches. As quantum technologies progress, building partnerships between sectors and encouraging information sharing among cyber security professionals can create a more fortified defense against threats. This vigilance will ensure that the promise of quantum cryptography as a truly secure communication method is realized in practice.

6.2 Side-Channel Attacks and Mitigations

Side-channel attacks are a significant threat to Quantum Key Distribution (QKD) systems, as they exploit unintended information leakage from the physical implementation of cryptographic systems. These attacks can occur through various channels, including timing information, power consumption patterns, electromagnetic emissions, and even sound. For instance, an attacker can analyze the time it takes for a QKD system to respond to a measurement or a cryptographic operation, allowing them to infer key information. Additionally, variations in power consumption during key generation and transmission can provide clues about the secrets being shared. The danger amplifies as the technology advances and attackers become more sophisticated, potentially using sophisticated techniques to breach the security of QKD systems. Even though the theoretical foundations of QKD provide a strong level of security, the practical implementation remains vulnerable due to side-channel attacks.

To mitigate the risks associated with these attacks, several strategies can be adopted. Implementing physical shielding around the QKD devices can significantly reduce the risk of eavesdropping through electromagnetic emissions, serving to contain the signals within the device. Furthermore, employing randomization techniques in the key generation process can help obscure patterns that might be detectable through timing or power analysis. Encryption inside secure hardware can also act as an additional layer of defense, as it can restrict access to the processed data and minimize leakage. Regular testing and updates of QKD systems are critical to ensure that potential vulnerabilities are identified and addressed promptly. Continuous monitoring for unusual patterns in power consumption or electromagnetic emissions can provide real-time alerts, allowing for quicker response to potential attacks. Building a robust security culture within organizations that embrace quantum cryptography will be key in harmonizing the novel approaches with existing security measures.

Professionals implementing QKD systems should pay close attention to these attack vectors and remain vigilant in their defenses, as the landscape of cyber threats is constantly evolving. Staying informed about the latest research on side-channel attacks and their mitigations will significantly enhance the resilience of QKD systems. Regular workshops and collaboration with other cyber security experts can facilitate knowledge sharing and best practices in defending against emerging threats. By prioritizing comprehensive security strategies and maintaining a proactive approach to threats, organizations can secure their quantum communication systems effectively.

6.3 Formal Security Proofs

Formal security proofs play a crucial role in establishing the reliability of quantum protocols, as they provide mathematical assurances that these systems operate as intended, even in the face of potential adversarial actions. In the realm of quantum cryptography, where principles differ markedly from classical systems, the stakes are notably high. By employing rigorous mathematical frameworks, researchers can validate the security claims of quantum key distribution (QKD) systems. This not only builds trust among users but also influences the adoption of these technologies in sensitive applications, such as governmental communication and financial transactions. Understanding the inherent mechanics of quantum systems leads to more robust protocols capable of withstanding attacks that exploit classical weaknesses.

Recent advancements in verification techniques have significantly enhanced our ability to ensure the security of quantum cryptographic protocols. Innovative methods, such as composability, allow for the evaluation of individual components within a system without compromising overall security. Techniques like game-based security models provide a sophisticated way to assess quantum protocols by simulating potential scenarios that could arise in real-world applications. These models enable researchers to identify vulnerabilities early in the development process, facilitating adjustments before deployment. Tools employing automated theorem proving are also gaining traction, offering scalability and efficiency in verifying complex quantum systems, thereby supporting the notion that formal proofs can adapt to the evolving landscape of quantum cryptography.

As practitioners in the field continue to explore these advancements, it is essential to remain updated on emerging verification methods. The confluence of formal security proofs and cutting-edge technologies presents an unprecedented opportunity to enhance the resilience of cryptographic systems. Cyber security professionals should actively engage with current research, participate in relevant forums, and consider integrating formal proofs into their security assessments to stay ahead in the fast-paced domain of quantum cryptography.

Chapter 7: Comparing Quantum and Classical Cryptography

7.1 Strengths and Weaknesses

Conducting a comparative analysis of strengths and weaknesses between quantum and classical cryptography reveals critical insights into their respective capabilities. Classical cryptography, which has been the backbone of digital security for decades, excels in terms of practicality and robust implementation across various systems. Its algorithms, such as RSA and AES, have withstood numerous attacks and are deeply entrenched in current security protocols. However, the chinks in this armour become apparent when considering the rising power of quantum computing. Classical methods rely on mathematical complexity that quantum computers can exploit, potentially breaking traditional encryption methods in the near future.

On the other hand, quantum cryptography presents a new paradigm in secure communication. The primary strength of quantum methods, particularly quantum key distribution (QKD), lies in the laws of quantum mechanics, which can guarantee the security of information exchange against eavesdropping. Unlike classical systems, where interception can lead to decrypted information, quantum systems can detect the presence of an intruder, rendering any attempted breach immediately obvious. Nevertheless, quantum cryptography faces its own challenges. Current implementations can be costly and require a level of infrastructure that may not be feasible for widespread adoption, especially in less economically developed regions. Moreover, while quantum methods promise higher security, they are not immune to future technological advancements that could address their inherent limitations.

Identifying where each approach excels and where they fall short is crucial for cyber security professionals looking to the future. Classical cryptography is already integrated into everyday applications and provides a level of security that meets the needs of many organizations. Yet, as quantum computers continue to develop, reliance on classical systems could pose a significant risk. Quantum cryptography shines in scenarios demanding the highest levels of security and where resources allow for advanced implementation, particularly in government, military, and critical infrastructure domains. It is essential for professionals in the field to remain informed about these evolving technologies and their implications for security architectures. Keeping abreast of advancements in both quantum and classical cryptography will not only aid in protecting sensitive data but also prepare organizations for the inevitable transition towards quantum-resistant systems as we move forward.

7.2 Use Cases for Each Approach

Different cryptographic methods serve distinct purposes and excel in various scenarios. Quantum cryptography, leveraging the principles of quantum mechanics, offers a level of security unattainable by classical methods. One specific use case for quantum cryptography is in securing communications in sensitive government or financial sectors. Institutions that handle highly confidential information, such as defense agencies or banks, require unbreakable encryption to protect against potential quantum attacks in the future. In contrast, classical cryptographic methods, such as RSA and AES, are still highly effective for a multitude of everyday applications, especially where quantum threats do not pose an immediate risk. For instance, classical encryption remains a reliable choice for securing data at rest on personal devices and databases. In this context, classical cryptography can provide robust protection without the need for complex quantum systems.

When selecting the appropriate cryptographic approach, a number of criteria must be taken into consideration. First, assess the level of threat your system faces. If the data is sensitive and potentially at risk of future quantum decryption, prioritizing quantum cryptographic methods would be prudent. Consider also the scalability of the solution. Quantum cryptography may not yet be as scalable or accessible for all types of organizations, particularly smaller businesses that may not require an advanced quantum solution immediately. Evaluate the performance requirements; classical methods generally provide faster processing speeds in the current infrastructure but may be outdated against emerging quantum capabilities. Ultimately, organizations should match their choice of cryptography with the nature of the information they protect, the immediate threats they face, and their readiness to invest in quantum technologies.

Being aware of the evolving landscape of cyber threats is essential for practitioners in the field. It's vital to stay informed about advancements in both quantum and classical cryptography and to assess the specific needs of each scenario. Forecasting the need for quantum-resistant solutions in your organization can facilitate a smoother transition as this technology matures. Regularly evaluating your cryptographic strategies and investing in ongoing education about emerging technologies will bolster defenses against the changing tides of cyber security.

7.3 The Future of Hybrid Systems

The future of hybrid systems that combine classical and quantum cryptography holds great promise for enhancing the security of digital communications. By integrating the strengths of both cryptographic methodologies, these systems can provide a multi-layered defense against evolving cyber threats. Classical cryptography, based on mathematical algorithms, is well-understood and widely implemented, while quantum cryptography introduces the principles of quantum mechanics to secure data transmission. In practice, a hybrid approach could enable organizations to benefit from the robustness of classical systems alongside the innovative security features of quantum technology. Such integration might allow for secure key distribution using quantum methods while employing established algorithms for data encryption and integrity, creating a comprehensive security framework capable of resisting even the most advanced cyber-attacks.

Hybrid cryptographic systems could significantly enhance security while leveraging existing infrastructure, making them appealing for organizations with substantial investments in traditional systems. By incorporating quantum key distribution into current environments, businesses could mitigate risks without the need for a complete overhaul of their existing systems. This transition may, for instance, involve integrating quantum-safe protocols into already established security frameworks, allowing for a gradual upgrade that is both cost-effective and less disruptive to daily operations. As industries face the increasing demands for secure communications in a digital age marked by rising sophistication in cyber threats, the implementation of hybrid systems represents a strategic advantage. Decision-makers should stay informed about advancements in both classical and quantum realms to ensure their organizations are not only prepared for the current landscape but also resilient against future challenges in cybersecurity.

Considering the ongoing advancements in quantum technology and its implications for cybersecurity, professionals in the field should actively explore hybrid options that could be tailored to their specific environments. Investing in training and fostering a culture of continuous learning within teams can prepare organizations to adeptly navigate the challenges of integrating these emerging technologies. Embracing hybrid systems not only positions an organization at the forefront of cybersecurity innovation but also builds a resilient defense mechanism, ready to face the complexities of an increasingly digital world.

Chapter 8: Quantum Cryptography in the Enterprise

8.1 Assessing Organizational Readiness

Evaluating whether an organization is prepared for the integration of quantum cryptography involves applying several frameworks that focus on technological, procedural, and cultural aspects. One effective framework is the technology readiness assessment, which scrutinizes the organization's current technology infrastructure, security practices, and overall adaptability to new innovations. It entails a thorough analysis of existing encryption methods, determining their strength against quantum threats. Moreover, integrating quantum cryptography necessitates investments in new technology and skill development. Assessing financial readiness is also vital; organizations must evaluate their budgets and resource allocation to engage effectively in quantum initiatives. Another framework involves assessing organizational culture, which involves understanding the readiness to embrace change, foster collaboration, and support continual learning to maintain a competitive edge in cybersecurity practices.

Several key factors and indicators of readiness help gauge an organization's position for adopting quantum cryptography. A significant indicator is the existing cybersecurity framework; organizations with robust security protocols are better equipped to transition to quantum methods. Furthermore, leadership support plays an essential role; when leaders prioritize quantum initiatives, it establishes a strategic direction and enhances motivation company-wide. Employee training and awareness are also crucial; organizations must ensure that their personnel possess a foundational understanding of quantum concepts, potential risks, and the benefits of adopting such technologies. Additionally, the organization's ability to collaborate with external experts and industry leaders can enhance its readiness, as it facilitates knowledge sharing and accelerates the integration process.

Monitoring these factors can provide valuable insights that guide decision-making. Organizations looking to prepare for quantum cryptography should initiate pilot projects aimed at experimenting with quantum key distribution and other foundational quantum applications. Engaging in partnerships with research institutions can help in understanding quantum technology better and understanding the potential impact on current systems. By initiating discussions about future policies regarding quantum adoption and addressing concerns related to regulatory compliance, organizations can create a more favourable environment for integration. A proactive approach focusing on these vital elements and engaging in continuous assessments will ensure readiness as quantum cryptography reshapes the landscape of cybersecurity.

8.2 Integrating Quantum Solutions into Existing Systems

Integrating quantum cryptographic solutions into legacy systems requires a well-thought-out strategy that addresses both technological and operational aspects. One of the first steps is to conduct a thorough assessment of existing infrastructures. This entails identifying which components of the legacy system are most critical and vulnerable to cyber threats. Legacy systems often have constraints such as outdated hardware and software, which may not support new quantum protocols. It is essential to evaluate how quantum key distribution (QKD) can be layered onto current security frameworks without causing significant disruption. Incrementally incorporating quantum components as an enhancement rather than a complete overhaul can ease the transition and reduce risks. Collaboration with key stakeholders in the organization can facilitate knowledge sharing and foster support for the integration process, making it less daunting.

However, the road to integration is not without its challenges. One significant hurdle is the lack of understanding of quantum technologies among many cybersecurity professionals, which may lead to resistance or hesitance regarding implementation. Training and education programs tailored for existing staff can effectively bridge this knowledge gap. Additionally, the unique nature of quantum cryptography presents interoperability issues with existing cryptographic protocols, as quantum-based solutions may require wholly different key management systems. Establishing robust protocols for the coexistence of classical and quantum systems is crucial. Testing phases that involve pilot programs can help in assessing the efficacy of these integrations and allow organizations to refine their approaches before a full-scale rollout. Developing a clear roadmap that outlines short, medium, and long-term integration goals can also help manage expectations and track progress.

The future of cybersecurity increasingly hinges on the successful melding of classical and quantum technologies. As organizations strive to future-proof their systems against the threats posed by quantum computing, it remains essential to maintain an adaptable mindset. Embracing the potential of quantum solutions while acknowledging the complexities of integration will ensure that cybersecurity professionals are not only prepared for today's challenges but are also building robust defenses for the evolving landscape ahead. A practical tip for organizations embarking on this journey is to cultivate relationships with quantum technology vendors and experts early on. Doing so can provide invaluable insights and resources as you navigate the complexities of integration and leverage the strengths of quantum encryption.

8.3 Training and Development for Security Teams

Training programs for security professionals in quantum cryptography are essential for equipping teams with the knowledge and skills needed to protect sensitive information in a rapidly evolving digital landscape. As quantum computing technologies advance, the traditional cryptographic methods currently in use may become vulnerable. Understanding the principles of quantum cryptography allows security professionals to develop and implement more secure communication methods that can withstand future threats. This involves not just theoretical knowledge, but practical skills that can be cultivated through well-structured training programs. Engaging in hands-on labs, simulations, and case studies relevant to quantum cryptography can significantly enhance a security professional's ability to respond effectively to breaches and vulnerabilities.

To enhance team competencies, security teams should have access to a variety of development resources and tools. This may include online courses specific to quantum technologies, interactive workshops, and up-to-date literature covering the latest research in quantum cryptography. Collaborating with academic institutions or Google Quantum AI, which focuses on understanding quantum algorithms, could provide invaluable insights and learning opportunities. Utilizing software tools that simulate quantum environments or cryptographic algorithms can enrich the team's understanding and readiness, allowing them to practice and implement strategies in controlled settings before facing real-world challenges. By fostering an environment of continuous learning and utilizing diverse resources, security teams can remain at the forefront of technological advances in quantum cryptography.

Creating a culture of growth within the security team is also necessary, where team members are encouraged to share their knowledge and experiences. This not only helps in retaining critical information but also builds resilience against emerging threats in cybersecurity. Regularly scheduled knowledge-sharing sessions or forums can be helpful in discussing new developments in quantum technology and practical applications of quantum cryptography in their specific fields. By valuing ongoing education and providing access to advanced resources, organizations can ensure their security teams are prepared for the challenges posed by quantum advancements.

Chapter 9: Policy and Regulatory Considerations

9.1 International Standards for Quantum Cryptography

International standards for quantum cryptography are evolving as the technology matures and as the need for robust cybersecurity measures becomes more critical. Currently, the most significant standards are guided by organizations such as the International Organization for Standardization (ISO), which are focusing on the development of the ISO/IEC 17829 standard concerning quantum key distribution (QKD). This standard aims to provide a framework for implementing and assessing QKD systems, ensuring interoperability and security. Additionally, the European Telecommunications Standards Institute (ETSI) has been proactive in creating standards that address the unique characteristics of quantum communications, emphasizing the importance of securing the quantum channel through which cryptographic keys are shared. As nations invest heavily in quantum technologies, active participation in these standards committees is essential for cybersecurity professionals to help influence and steer the direction of regulations that could shape the future landscape of secure communications.

The implications of these international standards stretch far beyond mere compliance; they represent a shift in how organizations approach cybersecurity. As quantum cryptographic methods gain acceptance, they will redefine the baseline for security protocols globally. Organizations that adopt these standards can be more confident in their defenses against cyber threats, as quantum cryptography offers the promise of unconditional security based on the laws of physics. This transition will also necessitate a re-evaluation of current cybersecurity strategies, requiring professionals to integrate quantum-ready technologies and practices into their infrastructure. The ability to exchange secure keys through quantum methods will become a competitive advantage, urging businesses to stay ahead in an arms race of technology advancements and threats. As quantum cryptography becomes mainstream, professionals will need to cultivate not only a solid understanding of these standards but also a proactive approach to implementing them in order to better protect sensitive information.

Diving into quantum cryptography today is not solely about understanding the technology but also about grasping the regulatory and compliance frameworks being put in place. Staying informed about these international standards and actively engaging with them is vital for cybersecurity professionals. By understanding the evolving landscape, they can anticipate changes, prepare their organizations for compliance, and advocate for the best practices that harness the full potential of quantum security. Committing to ongoing education and participation in discussions surrounding quantum standards will empower professionals to lead in this crucial area of cybersecurity.

9.2 Compliance and Legal Implications

Deploying quantum cryptographic solutions introduces a range of legal and compliance requirements that organizations must navigate. As the technology evolves, regulators are starting to catch up with the implications of quantum capabilities on data privacy and security. Organizations must remain vigilant to meet these regulatory standards, including but not limited to data protection laws like GDPR in Europe, HIPAA in the healthcare sector in the United States, and various other national security frameworks. These regulations often mandate that organizations take appropriate measures to protect sensitive data, and quantum cryptographic solutions, with their potential to offer unprecedented levels of security, could be an attractive option. However, it is essential to ensure these solutions are implemented in a manner compliant with the specific requirements of the relevant jurisdictions. In many cases, this involves carrying out thorough risk assessments and implementing robust governance frameworks to ensure ongoing compliance as the technology and regulations continue to evolve.

Potential liability issues and risks are foremost in the minds of organizations considering quantum cryptography. The deployment of these solutions introduces unique challenges, particularly concerning the reliability and integrity of the encryption methods used. If a quantum cryptographic system fails to protect data as anticipated, organizations could face significant legal repercussions, including liability for breaches of sensitive information. Additionally, there are concerns regarding the potential misuse of quantum capabilities by malicious actors, which poses a real threat to industry sectors that handle critical infrastructure. Engaging with legal experts who specialize in cybersecurity law can help organizations understand their exposure and assist in drafting contracts and guidelines that clearly define the scope and limits of liability. Risk management must, therefore, include not only technological assessments but also legal projections, ensuring that companies are prepared for a swiftly changing landscape in which quantum technology plays a central role. Awareness of these legal pitfalls will allow professionals to take preventive measures that safeguard their organizations from potential crises.

Staying informed about the evolving legal landscape surrounding quantum cryptography is crucial for any cybersecurity professional. Regular training sessions focusing on current regulations and potential ramifications of quantum technology, in addition to fostering collaborations with legal advisors, can significantly mitigate risks. Utilizing the latest resources and industry reports will also enhance understanding, enabling professionals to lead their organizations confidently into the era of quantum security.

9.3 Ethical Considerations in Data Protection

The introduction of quantum cryptography into the field of data protection brings with it a set of intricate ethical dimensions that must be thoroughly considered. As this technology advances, it promises to revolutionize how we secure data by offering an unprecedented level of security through principles rooted in the laws of quantum mechanics. However, ethical dilemmas arise when considering the potential for misuse. For example, organizations might employ quantum encryption not just for legitimate protection of sensitive information but also to exploit this superior security in a manner that undermines privacy rights. The ethical deployment of quantum cryptography necessitates a dialogue about who has access to such powerful tools and how they are wielded. This is particularly crucial as governments and corporations may prioritize their interests over individual rights. Professionals in cyber security must engage with these ethical concerns, ensuring that technological advancements do not come at the expense of the fundamental rights of individuals. Establishing a framework that promotes responsible usage and discourages unethical practices is essential to fostering trust in quantum encryption technologies.

The role of ethics in shaping policy frameworks for cybersecurity cannot be overstated, particularly in an era where technologies evolve rapidly. As we move towards a future where quantum cryptography might be standard practice, it becomes vital to weave ethical considerations into the fabric of cybersecurity policies. This involves not only crafting regulations that govern the use of such technologies but also facilitating public discourse to create awareness around their implications. Policymakers and cybersecurity professionals must collaborate to create an ethical foundation that guides the development and implementation of these technologies. Transparency, accountability, and respect for user privacy should be core principles in the formation of these frameworks. Emphasizing ethical standards helps ensure that all stakeholders, including users and organizations, understand their responsibilities and the potential consequences of their actions in the digital realm. Building a culture of ethics within the cybersecurity community will support a secure environment where innovative technologies like quantum cryptography can thrive without compromising individual freedoms.

Staying informed about the ethical implications of emerging technologies can enhance a cybersecurity professional's capability to address these issues proactively. It is advisable to engage in ongoing education on themes of privacy, security, and ethics as they relate to new tools like quantum cryptography. Regular discussions with colleagues and participation in forums dedicated to cybersecurity ethics can provide valuable insights and strengthen your understanding of the ethical landscape within which you operate.

Chapter 10: Challenges in Quantum Cryptography Deployment

10.1 Technology Maturity and Commercial Viability

Quantum cryptographic technologies are evolving rapidly, with varying maturity levels across the market. Current implementations, such as quantum key distribution (QKD), have made significant strides, especially in laboratory settings and specific pilot projects. These technologies utilize the principles of quantum mechanics to ensure secure communications, fundamentally changing the landscape of cyber security. Yet, their maturity in commercial applications remains uneven. While some organizations have begun deploying quantum encryption solutions in niche areas like defense and financial services, widespread adoption faces hurdles. These include the high costs of quantum systems, the need for compatible infrastructure, and understanding the nuances of quantum principles. As research continues and new standards emerge, we are likely to see increased readiness in consumer and enterprise solutions, but the transition requires careful navigation through the existing technological ecosystem.

From a business perspective, the commercial viability of quantum solutions hinges on several key factors. First, companies must evaluate the return on investment (ROI) of implementing quantum cryptography against existing security solutions. Although quantum technologies offer unparalleled security, especially against future threats like quantum computing, organizations must assess whether the current risks justify the investment. Furthermore, businesses researching quantum solutions face challenges related to scalability, integration with legacy systems, and the training of personnel. However, as the landscape of cyber threats evolves, there is an opportunity for early adopters to gain a competitive advantage by enhancing their security protocols with quantum solutions. Establishing partnerships with research institutions and technology providers can also facilitate a smoother transition into quantum cryptography, enabling organizations to maintain resilience against emerging vulnerabilities.

As you explore the implications of quantum cryptography for your organization, it is crucial to stay updated on the latest advancements and regulatory frameworks. Regularly attending industry conferences and participating in professional networks can provide valuable insights into best practices and emerging trends in quantum security.

10.2 Infrastructure and Cost Barriers

Implementing quantum cryptography faces significant infrastructure challenges and cost barriers that inhibit its widespread adoption. Quantum key distribution (QKD), a cornerstone of quantum cryptography, requires specialized hardware to generate, transmit, and receive quantum keys. This hardware often relies on advanced technologies, such as superconducting circuits and photon detectors. These technologies are not only costly to develop but also mandate a considerable investment in the supporting infrastructure. Furthermore, existing telecommunications networks may lack compatibility with quantum systems, forcing organizations to consider substantial upgrades or replacements. Moreover, the need for secure transmission lines, such as fibre optic cables designed for quantum applications, adds an additional layer of complexity in terms of installation and maintenance, further inflating costs.

To overcome these barriers, organizations can explore several potential solutions. Collaborative partnerships between academia, industry, and government can drive research and development efforts aimed at reducing the costs associated with quantum technologies. By pooling resources and expertise, stakeholders can work together to create more affordable solutions, potentially benefitting from shared infrastructure development. Additionally, investing in hybrid systems that combine classical and quantum cryptography can offer a transitional pathway, allowing organizations to leverage existing technologies while gradually incorporating quantum elements. Standardizing protocols and components across the industry may also help streamline costs and encourage the adoption of quantum cryptography. Ultimately, fostering an ecosystem where innovation can flourish while addressing cost and infrastructure challenges is crucial for the future of quantum cryptography.

Staying informed about advancements in quantum technology and participating in collaborative initiatives can empower cyber security professionals to take proactive steps toward integrating quantum cryptography within their security frameworks, ensuring they are prepared for the next wave of cyber threats.

10.3 Educating the Market about Quantum Solutions

Understanding market education on quantum cryptographic solutions is essential for the growth of secure communications in our digital landscape. As quantum technologies develop, so do the potential threats to our current cybersecurity protocols. Traditional encryption methods may become obsolete in the face of quantum computing. Therefore, educating stakeholders about the importance of quantum cryptography is critical. Organizations need to grasp the fundamentals of how quantum cryptography works, such as the principles of superposition and entanglement, which provide unparalleled security advantages. A well-informed market is better equipped to adopt quantum solutions, ensuring a smoother transition and greater protection of sensitive data.

Raising awareness and understanding among stakeholders can be achieved through several strategic approaches. One effective method is to conduct workshops and seminars aimed at cybersecurity professionals and organizational leaders. These events can serve as platforms for discussing the implications of quantum computing on cryptographic practices and showcasing real-world applications of quantum cryptography. Providing accessible educational materials, such as white papers, webinars, and case studies, can also enhance understanding. Building partnerships with academic institutions can help leverage research as well as foster collaboration for developing innovative quantum solutions. Engaging in discussions within industry forums will further allow cybersecurity professionals to share insights, address concerns, and promote a proactive stance in adopting quantum technologies.

To lean into a future of true cybersecurity, explore opportunities to engage with quantum technology experts. Inviting them to speak at your organization can provide valuable perspectives and deepen the collective understanding of quantum cryptography's importance.

Keeping abreast of ongoing research and advancements in this field will empower cybersecurity professionals to make informed decisions that ultimately enhance their protective measures against potential quantum threats.

Chapter 11: Future Trends in Quantum Cryptography

11.1 Evolution of Quantum Algorithms

The landscape of quantum algorithms is evolving rapidly, particularly in their potential impact on cryptography. Traditional cryptographic systems rely heavily on mathematical problems that are currently intractable for classical computers, such as factoring large integers or solving discrete logarithms. However, quantum algorithms like Shor's algorithm have demonstrated the ability to solve these problems exponentially faster than classical algorithms, raising significant concerns for the security of widely used encryption methods. As quantum computing technology matures, the implications for cryptography become increasingly urgent. Cryptographers are now faced with the critical challenge of developing quantum-resistant algorithms to safeguard sensitive information against potential threats posed by quantum computers. The urgent need for these solutions necessitates a deep understanding of both quantum mechanics and classical cryptography, as well as the development of new mathematical frameworks that can withstand quantum attacks.

Looking to the future, the research directions in quantum algorithm development are both promising and challenging. Researchers are now exploring a variety of approaches, such as investigating new quantum algorithms specifically designed for optimization problems, machine learning applications, and cryptographic protocols. The advent of hybrid quantum-classical algorithms is also an area of keen interest, as these could leverage the strengths of both types of computing to tackle complex problems more efficiently. Furthermore, the growing field of quantum communication protocols, such as quantum key distribution (QKD), requires rigorous research to ensure that these methods can be both practical and secure in real-world applications. With continuous advancements in quantum technology and computing capabilities, it is crucial for cybersecurity professionals to remain vigilant and adaptable, actively engaging with the latest developments to effectively mitigate risks. Staying informed about emerging quantum algorithms and their potential applications is vital for developing robust cryptographic strategies in this new era of cybersecurity.

One practical approach for cybersecurity professionals is to start integrating quantum risk assessments into their security frameworks. This means evaluating which cryptographic systems are vulnerable to quantum attacks and planning the transition to quantum-resistant algorithms. By doing so, organizations can not only prepare for the challenges posed by quantum computing but also build a more secure and resilient cybersecurity posture for the future.

11.2 Integration with Emerging Technologies

Quantum cryptography has emerged as a groundbreaking field that promises to enhance the security of data transmission in a world increasingly reliant on technology. When integrated with advanced technologies such as artificial intelligence (AI) and blockchain, quantum cryptography can create a robust framework for securing communications. AI algorithms can analyze large datasets and detect anomalies faster than human capabilities, making them ideal for identifying potential cyber threats. Meanwhile, blockchain technology can enhance data integrity and transparency by recording transactions in an immutable way. The combination of these technologies allows for quantum key distribution (QKD) to be employed in securing the transmission of keys necessary for encryption. This synergy not only fortifies the security of sensitive data but also enhances trust in digital ecosystems, paving the way for safer interactions in finance, healthcare, and other critical sectors.

Collaboration among these technologies can yield substantial benefits in terms of security and operational efficiency. When organizations leverage AI for real-time data analysis in conjunction with quantum cryptography, they can proactively address vulnerabilities before they are exploited. The predictive capabilities of AI models can be instrumental in anticipating cyber threats, while quantum cryptography ensures that any communication remains unbreakable. Additionally, integrating blockchain can streamline operational processes by automating secure transactions without intermediary intervention, which reduces the risk of human error. Companies that adopt this collaborative approach find themselves not only more secure against cyber threats but also positioned to operate more efficiently, enhancing their overall resilience against attack.

For cyber security professionals looking to the future, it is crucial to understand the potential of these technologies. Continuous education on quantum cryptography, alongside the development of AI and blockchain applications, will remain imperative. Organizations that invest in these integrated solutions are more likely to achieve a formidable defense against emerging cyber threats, ultimately fostering a safer digital environment.

11.3 Predictions for Future Developments

The landscape of quantum cryptography and cybersecurity is poised for transformative growth as we enter a new era of technology. As quantum computers advance in power and capability, the encryption protocols that have long secured our communications and transactions must evolve. It is anticipated that quantum-resistant algorithms will emerge, developed specifically to withstand the unique threats posed by quantum computation. The transition to quantum key distribution (QKD) will become mainstream, as organizations seek to utilize its inherent security advantages, leveraging the principles of quantum mechanics to create invulnerable key exchanges. Additionally, we may see the development of new standards in cryptographic practices, aiming to unify quantum security measures globally and ensure a standardized approach that organizations can adopt. As the demand for secure data transmission increases, education regarding quantum cybersecurity will also become crucial, with enterprises likely investing in protocols that offer training and awareness to foster environments resilient against quantum-enabled attacks.

The implications of these developments will be significant for organizations across all sectors. As quantum cryptography technologies become mainstream, companies will need to reassess their cybersecurity frameworks, potentially shifting to robust, quantum-safe protocols to protect sensitive information. The financial sector, which deals with vast amounts of data and requires the highest levels of security, will likely lead the charge in adopting quantum encryption methods. Organizations may also start to see changes in compliance and regulatory requirements, pushing for stricter guidelines that incorporate quantum resilience measures. Furthermore, partnerships with quantum technology firms may become a strategic imperative, as businesses will seek to leverage specialized expertise in integrating quantum solutions into their existing infrastructures. Investments in cybersecurity infrastructures will expand, not only to safeguard against traditional threats but also to combat potential vulnerabilities associated with quantum advancements. This evolving landscape requires cyber security professionals to stay informed, adapt swiftly, and adopt proactive measures to mitigate risks associated with quantum advancements.

One practical tip for cybersecurity professionals is to begin evaluating current cryptographic methods against emerging quantum threats. Organizations should start pilot projects to explore quantum key distribution and other quantum-resistant solutions, allowing them to become early adopters in a rapidly changing technological environment. Engaging in collaborative research and development with academic institutions and industry leaders can also foster innovation and help create tailored solutions to meet the unique security demands of the future.

Chapter 12: Real-World Case Studies

12.1 Successful Implementations of QKD

Notable successful implementations of Quantum Key Distribution (QKD) are paving the way for the future of secure communications globally. One exemplary case is the Tokyo QKD Network, which has been operational since 2010 and uses a fibre optic system to transmit qubits over long distances. This network spans the city of Tokyo and facilitates secure transmissions between major banks and government institutions. In Europe, the SECOQC project, established in Austria, has demonstrated a successful QKD implementation across ten nodes, enabling secure communication between different entities within the European Union. Similarly, the Chinese quantum satellite, Micius, launched in 2016, has showcased the ability to conduct QKD over thousands of kilometres, providing real-time encryption capabilities for satellite communications. These implementations illustrate the practical application of QKD in protecting sensitive information against potential threats.

Key takeaways from these successful QKD implementations emphasize the importance of infrastructure and collaboration among various stakeholders. One significant lesson learned is the need for a robust framework that combines both quantum and classical cryptographic methods, allowing for a smoother integration into existing systems. Additionally, the projects highlighted the necessity of extensive testing under real-world conditions to identify potential vulnerabilities. The involvement of academic institutions, government bodies, and private sectors has proven critical in fostering innovation and driving QKD advancements. Establishing clear regulatory frameworks and standard protocols also emerged as vital, enabling interoperability and ensuring compliance with international security standards. Sharing knowledge and experiences among these diverse stakeholders contributes to building trust and promotes wider adoption of QKD technologies.

For professionals in the field of cyber security, staying informed about these successful implementations is crucial. Engaging with ongoing research and emerging technologies can enhance understanding and foster preparedness for rapid advancements in quantum cryptography. A practical tip is to start evaluating current systems and considering potential upgrades that incorporate elements of quantum technology, ensuring a proactive approach to future cyber security challenges.

12.2 Lessons Learned from Early Adoption

Early adopters of quantum cryptography have provided invaluable insights into the technology's potential and limitations. Their experiences highlight how critical it is to understand the fundamentals of quantum mechanics as they relate to cryptographic protocols. One significant lesson is the importance of robust infrastructure to support quantum key distribution (QKD) systems. Many early implementations faced challenges due to network congestion and inadequate hardware capabilities, which led to failures in maintaining secure key exchange. Additionally, issues surrounding the integration of quantum systems with existing classical systems emphasized the necessity for thorough planning and testing during the deployment stages. Early adopters also recognized the value of collaboration with academic and research institutions, which can help refine algorithms and protocols before scaling them for real-world use. This cooperative approach not only accelerates technological maturity but also reduces the risk of unforeseen vulnerabilities.

However, the journey of early adopters is not without pitfalls. One common mistake was overestimating the security guarantees offered by quantum cryptography. While the theoretical underpinnings of quantum mechanics promise higher levels of security, real-world implementations can still be vulnerable to attacks if not carefully designed. Moreover, neglecting to address the human element in cybersecurity often led to breaches. Social engineering tactics remain effective, and organizations must educate their personnel on weaknesses that could compromise even the most advanced encryption methods. Another issue was the failure to leverage existing cryptographic knowledge, as some adopters approached quantum cryptography as a completely new field, rather than building on the foundations of established cryptographic practices. By recognizing and avoiding these pitfalls, organizations can better safeguard their quantum implementations and ensure a more seamless transition to this innovative technology.

Pragmatic advice stems from these lessons. Organizations planning to adopt quantum cryptography should invest in extensive training for their technical teams, ensuring they possess a solid understanding of both the quantum concepts and the current cybersecurity landscape. This knowledge is crucial when tailoring quantum solutions to specific needs. Building partnerships with research institutions can also provide access to emerging best practices and ongoing advancements. Furthermore, a commitment to continuous monitoring and evaluation of systems is essential, allowing for prompt identification and mitigation of vulnerabilities as they arise. By fostering a well-rounded approach that considers technical, human, and collaborative factors, organizations can optimize their strategies and enhance their overall cybersecurity posture.

12.3 Impacts on National Security and Infrastructure

The advent of quantum cryptography introduces profound implications for national security efforts. At its core, quantum cryptography leverages the principles of quantum mechanics to create secure communication channels that are theoretically immune to interception. This breakthrough is particularly vital in an age where traditional cryptographic methods face mounting threats from quantum computers capable of breaking existing encryption standards. By incorporating quantum cryptographic techniques, nations can significantly enhance the confidentiality of sensitive communications, including governmental and military exchanges. The ability to generate a secure quantum key that is shared only between the sender and receiver ensures that any attempt to eavesdrop would not only be detected but would also render the transmitted information void. This capability fundamentally shifts the paradigm of information security, making it a crucial element in protecting national interests against espionage and cyber threats.

Moreover, quantum solutions can play a pivotal role in safeguarding critical infrastructure. Systems such as power grids, transportation networks, and financial institutions are increasingly reliant on interconnected technologies, rendering them vulnerable to cyberattacks. Implementing quantum cryptographic protocols across these infrastructures can protect data integrity and operator communications against unauthorized access. For example, in the energy sector, quantum-secured communications can help ensure that grid management systems remain operational even in the face of aggressive cyber intrusions. Similarly, using quantum encryption to secure financial transactions can bolster trust and safety in digital finance, reducing the likelihood of breaches that could lead to financial instability. As a result, adopting quantum cryptography across various critical sectors not only enhances privacy but also fortifies national resilience against evolving cyber threats.

The integration of quantum cryptography into national security and critical infrastructure systems demands continuous innovation and adaptation. As cyber threats evolve, so must the strategies to combat them. Staying informed about advancements in quantum technologies and understanding their practical applications can provide cyber security professionals with a strategic edge. Investing in training and resources to implement these quantum solutions will be essential in fostering a more secure future.

Chapter 13: Quantum Computers and Their Impact on Cyber Security

13.1 Understanding Quantum Computing Principles

Quantum computing is grounded in principles that diverge significantly from classical computing. At the heart of quantum computing are quantum bits, or qubits, which differ from traditional bits that exist solely as a zero or a one. Qubits, however, can exist in a superposition of states, meaning they can hold both values simultaneously. This property allows quantum computers to process a vast amount of information in parallel, greatly enhancing computational power for specific types of problems. Furthermore, qubits can be entangled, linking their states regardless of the distance separating them. This entanglement facilitates remarkably deep relationships between qubits, leading to potentially faster processing speeds and complex problem-solving capabilities that classical computers struggle to achieve. Understanding these principles helps frame the need for a shift in how we secure information in an era where quantum technologies are becoming more prevalent.

The implications of quantum computing for cybersecurity are profound and potentially transformational. Traditional encryption methods, such as RSA and ECC, rely on the difficulty of problems like factoring large integers or computing discrete logarithms. Quantum computers could solve these problems exponentially faster than classical computers using algorithms like Shor's Algorithm, rendering existing encryption methods vulnerable to being broken. This reality necessitates the exploration of quantum-resistant cryptographic methods that can withstand the capabilities of quantum computers. Additionally, quantum key distribution (QKD) emerges as a promising technique to enhance secure communications. It leverages the properties of quantum mechanics to enable two parties to create a shared secret key, ensuring that any interception of the key would alter the quantum states involved, signalling a breach. As cybersecurity professionals, staying informed about these advancements is crucial in adapting and evolving our current security paradigms to truly safeguard sensitive data in the quantum era.

As quantum technologies continue to advance, a proactive approach is essential. Engaging in continuous education and research in quantum cryptography, as well as evaluating the current cryptographic measures in place, can prepare cybersecurity professionals to tackle the challenges posed by quantum computing. Regularly updating and testing current encryption methods against emerging quantum threats will be necessary to maintain a robust security posture in this dynamic landscape.

13.2 Potential Threats to Classical Cryptography

Quantum computers present a unique challenge to classical encryption methods, which have been the foundation of secure communication for decades. Unlike traditional computers, quantum computers can process vast amounts of data simultaneously due to the principles of superposition and entanglement. This ability makes them particularly adept at executing algorithms that can break classical cryptographic systems. For example, Shor's algorithm can factor large numbers exponentially faster than any known classical algorithm. This implies that widely used encryption schemes, such as RSA and ECC, could be rendered insecure almost overnight once sufficiently powerful quantum computers become available. Consequently, the very codes that protect sensitive information, from financial transactions to national security communications, may be vulnerable to decryption, leading to significant concerns for data privacy and integrity.

The timeline for when these threats may become a reality is still uncertain but is a topic of keen interest among cybersecurity professionals. Experts suggest that while small-scale quantum computers have already been implemented in research labs, it may still take decades before they are robust enough to compromise classical encryption systems on a large scale. Estimates vary, but many believe that within the next 10 to 20 years, we could witness the advent of quantum computers capable of challenging existing cryptographic protocols. Organizations are beginning to recognize this impending threat and are considering proactive measures such as developing quantum-resistant algorithms. Though we have time to prepare, the transition to more secure cryptographic methods needs to begin now in order to safeguard information against potential quantum attacks in the near future.

Keeping abreast of developments in quantum computing and cryptography is crucial for cybersecurity professionals. One practical step to take right now is to participate in forums and training opportunities focused on post-quantum cryptography. This not only ensures you stay informed about the latest research and trends but also positions you to contribute to your organization's strategic planning in response to the evolving landscape of cybersecurity threats.

13.3 The Role of Quantum Cryptography in Defense

Quantum cryptography offers groundbreaking solutions to the emerging threats posed by advances in quantum computing. As quantum computers evolve, they possess the potential to break widely used cryptographic systems, which rely on complex mathematical problems. Quantum cryptography, particularly Quantum Key Distribution (QKD), provides a protective mechanism by utilizing the principles of quantum mechanics. It ensures that any attempt to intercept or measure the quantum bits (qubits) involved in the key distribution process is detectable. This detection serves as a safeguard, enabling secure communication channels that traditional encryption methods cannot guarantee. By harnessing the nature of quantum states, organizations can establish a new paradigm of security, fortifying sensitive information against both current and future quantum threats.

Integrating quantum defenses into existing cybersecurity frameworks requires strategic initiatives that align with technological innovations and threat landscapes. Organizations should begin by conducting comprehensive assessments to understand their vulnerability to quantum attacks. Following this, investing in research and collaboration with quantum technologists will be essential to stay ahead of quantum threats. Developing and implementing robust training programs for cybersecurity professionals to familiarize them with quantum concepts and practical applications will ensure that the workforce is equipped to leverage these advanced security measures. Collaborating with government and industry counterparts can also facilitate the sharing of knowledge and best practices, promoting a unified defense strategy. As quantum cryptography evolves, it is crucial to maintain an adaptable posture, ready to incorporate new advancements in cold regional and international cybersecurity policies.

The adoption of quantum cryptography should not be seen as a far-off ambition but as a vital step toward enhancing cybersecurity today. Organizations should begin identifying critical areas where quantum-resistant measures can be implemented, thus paving the way for a future-proof defense strategy. Establishing pilot projects using QKD can help demonstrate its practicality and effectiveness, encouraging a broader acceptance among stakeholders wary of new technologies. As the threat landscape transforms, organizations that embrace quantum cryptography not only enhance their security posture but also lead the charge toward a more secure digital future.

Chapter 14: Collaboration and Research in Quantum Cryptography

14.1 Key Research Institutions and Initiatives

Leading research institutions such as MIT's Research Laboratory of Electronics and the University of California, Berkeley are at the forefront of advancements in quantum cryptography. They contribute significantly to the development of quantum key distribution (QKD) protocols, pushing the boundaries of secure communication methods. Institutions like the University of Waterloo's Institute for Quantum Computing and the European Organization for Nuclear Research (CERN) are also pivotal in exploring the implications of quantum mechanics for cryptographic applications. Research initiatives from these institutions focus not only on theoretical aspects but also on practical implementations that can eventually secure sensitive information against potential quantum computing threats, ensuring a proactive approach to cybersecurity challenges.

Emerging research initiatives such as the Quantum Internet Alliance and the Quantum Computing and Communication Institute are reshaping the landscape of quantum cryptography. These initiatives aim to integrate quantum technologies into existing infrastructures, facilitating the development of a quantum internet that promises unprecedented levels of security and efficiency. Additionally, collaboration between industry leaders and academic institutions is fostering a rapid exchange of ideas, resulting in novel quantum algorithms and advanced hardware solutions that are essential for the practical deployment of quantum cryptography. This collaborative approach is crucial in addressing challenges such as scalability and interoperability, paving the way for mainstream adoption of quantum-secure systems.

Staying engaged with these research developments and initiatives is crucial for cybersecurity professionals. Understanding the latest advancements can provide insights into how to enhance current cybersecurity frameworks and prepare for the potential disruptions caused by quantum technologies. Familiarizing oneself with the leading institutions and their projects can help professionals identify key trends and emerging threats, ultimately facilitating a more robust and forward-thinking cybersecurity posture.

14.2 Public-Private Partnerships

Public-private partnerships (PPPs) play a crucial role in propelling quantum cryptographic research and its practical applications. By merging the innovation and agility of private enterprises with the stability and public interest mandate of government entities, these collaborations are essential for overcoming the complex challenges in the field of quantum cryptography. The fast-paced nature of technological advancements necessitates an environment where shared expertise can flourish. Government agencies often bring regulatory insight and long-term funding, while private firms contribute cutting-edge research capabilities and market-driven approaches. This synergy not only accelerates the development of quantum technologies but also establishes standards and protocols essential for widespread implementation. Such partnerships can foster a research ecosystem that propels quantum key distribution (QKD) and other quantum communication methods into practical use, enhancing data security significantly.

Several case studies illustrate the success of these collaborative models. One noteworthy example is the collaboration between various U.S. national laboratories and private tech companies, which has led to breakthrough innovations in quantum networks. The Department of Energy has actively engaged private firms specializing in quantum information science, driving projects that integrate quantum computing with existing cybersecurity frameworks. Another significant initiative is Europe's Quantum Flagship program, which involves extensive cooperation between universities, research institutes, and businesses across multiple sectors. This program has not only catalysed advancements in quantum technology but also created a robust training environment for future professionals in the field. These successful case studies reinforce the idea that strategic alliances between public and private sectors can leverage diverse strengths, yielding results that would be challenging for either side to achieve independently.

Engagement in public-private partnerships presents a pathway for cyber security professionals to stay at the forefront of quantum cryptographic advancements. Professionals are encouraged to seek out avenues for collaboration, whether through research initiatives or industry consortia, as these partnerships can offer unique insights into emerging threats and solutions. Understanding the landscape of quantum cryptography and its integration into the broader cyber security framework will require proactive participation in these collaborative efforts. By fostering relationships across sectors, professionals not only contribute to the development of secure quantum technologies but also enhance their own expertise and career prospects in a rapidly evolving field.

14.3 Challenges in Collaborative Research

Collaborative research in quantum cryptography often encounters several key challenges that can impede progress and innovation. One significant issue is the disparity in expertise among partners. Different research teams may possess varying levels of knowledge and understanding regarding quantum mechanics, cryptographic protocols, or cybersecurity principles. This gap can lead to miscommunication, where assumptions are made based on differing levels of expertise. Additionally, the complexity of quantum technologies creates a steep learning curve, requiring constant education and discussion to ensure all collaborators are aligned. Another challenge is the integration of diverse research methodologies and frameworks, which can clash when teams attempt to merge their approaches to problem-solving. Variations in experimental design, data collection, and analysis practices can disrupt workflow and generate friction among collaborators. Furthermore, intellectual property concerns often arise when multiple institutions are involved. Researchers may fear that their contributions could be misappropriated, leading to hesitance in sharing critical findings or methodologies. These combined factors can hinder both communication and trust, ultimately impacting the success of collaborative efforts.

To address these challenges and foster effective collaboration in quantum cryptography research, several strategies can be implemented. Establishing clear communication channels is paramount. Regular meetings and discussions can help bridge the knowledge gap, ensuring that all team members are on the same page. Utilizing collaborative tools and platforms that allow for real-time sharing of ideas, data, and feedback can streamline communication and help create a unified understanding of project goals. Building a culture of trust is also essential. This can be achieved by setting clear expectations regarding intellectual property rights upfront and ensuring that all collaborators feel secure in the sharing of their insights. Developing a shared language or framework for discussing complex concepts can further enhance mutual understanding and collaboration. It can be beneficial to establish joint training sessions where team members can learn from one another, fostering a deeper appreciation of each other's expertise. By combining these approaches, research teams can create an environment conducive to collaboration, driving innovation within the field of quantum cryptography.

Being proactive in addressing these challenges can significantly enhance the outcomes of collaborative research. Cybersecurity professionals engaging in quantum cryptography projects should prioritize the establishment of a strong foundation of communication and trust. By recognizing and addressing disparities in expertise and understanding the importance of a unified approach, researchers can cultivate an environment that leads to breakthroughs and advancements in cybersecurity. Effective collaboration does not happen by chance; it requires intentional effort and elevated awareness of potential challenges.

Chapter 15: Conclusion and Final Thoughts

15.1 Summary of Key Insights

This book has explored the transformative potential of quantum cryptography, emphasizing its role as a groundbreaking technology that could redefine the landscape of cybersecurity. At its core, quantum cryptography leverages the principles of quantum mechanics to facilitate secure communication, where the mere act of eavesdropping on a quantum channel alters the transmitted data, alerting the parties involved. This unique feature of quantum key distribution (QKD) makes it inherently secure against threats posed by traditional computational methods and even future quantum computers, which could potentially break established encryption standards. The insights shared throughout this book highlight the necessity of integrating quantum technologies into current security protocols to stay ahead of adversarial tactics that exploit classical vulnerabilities.

For cybersecurity professionals, understanding the implications of quantum cryptography is critical. Staying informed about the developments in quantum technologies can position security leaders to better implement robust systems that incorporate quantum solutions. The transition from classical to quantum-safe algorithms must be a strategic priority, ensuring that organizations are prepared for the advent of quantum computing capabilities. It is also essential to foster collaborations with researchers and technology providers specializing in quantum cryptography to gain insights into emerging tools and frameworks. As the landscape of cybersecurity evolves, proactive engagement with quantum cryptography will not only shield sensitive information but will also enhance the overall resilience of cybersecurity infrastructures.

Keeping an eye on regulatory changes surrounding quantum technology is equally important. As governments and standards bodies begin to recognize the significance of quantum-safe solutions, cybersecurity professionals must ensure compliance and adapt their practices accordingly. Continuous education and training in quantum cryptography will empower professionals to effectively integrate these innovations into their existing security architectures. This approach not only maximizes defenses against potential threats but also leverages cutting-edge technology to foster confidence in the security of digital communication. Adapting early to quantum cryptography will be a competitive advantage in the increasingly complex field of cybersecurity.

15.2 The Ongoing Journey in Quantum Cryptography

Ongoing developments in quantum cryptography continue to push the boundaries of secure communication. Researchers are making significant strides in various aspects of this technology, focusing on enhancing protocols such as Quantum Key Distribution (QKD) and exploring new quantum communication channels. With various implementations of QKD, including free-space and fibre-optic systems, the quest for perfect encryption is evolving. Upscaling these systems for real-world applications remains a challenge, yet numerous experiments demonstrate the feasibility of quantum networks. The European Union's Quantum Communication Infrastructure project and similar initiatives indicate a strong commitment to advancing this field, with the potential for global quantum networks that could transform data security standards worldwide. As understanding deepens, the theoretical framework is undergoing continuous refinement, paving the way for novel algorithms that leverage quantum principles to combat emerging cyber threats.

Adaptability in security strategies will be crucial as quantum cryptography matures. Cybersecurity professionals must recognize that the landscape of threats evolves rapidly. Legacy systems often fail to integrate emerging technologies, rendering traditional security measures inadequate. The ability to pivot in response to newfound vulnerabilities and advances in quantum computing is essential. This adaptability should not only encompass the implementation of quantum-resilient algorithms but also the integration of quantum technologies into existing infrastructures. Organizations must remain vigilant and invest in training to ensure that their teams are equipped to handle both current and next-generation security challenges. By fostering a culture of continuous learning and embracing change, cybersecurity experts can safeguard systems against potential breaches, maintaining the integrity of sensitive information in a quantum-enabled future.

Furthermore, collaboration within the cybersecurity community is vital for tackling the complexities of quantum cryptography. Sharing insights, best practices, and research advancements can accelerate progress in this field. As professionals work together to establish common standards and protocols, they lay a solid foundation for the ethical and practical implementation of quantum technologies. Regular conferences and workshops dedicated to quantum cryptography can enhance understanding and stimulate innovative ideas. By actively participating in these collaborative efforts, cybersecurity professionals can position themselves at the forefront of this transformative journey, ensuring that their strategies remain at the cutting edge of security and capable of addressing both present and future threats.

15.3 Call to Action for Cyber Security Professionals

Engagement with quantum cryptography is no longer a futuristic concept; it is becoming a crucial reality for cybersecurity professionals. As quantum computing evolves, its implications on conventional encryption methods cannot be overstated. Traditional cybersecurity protocols are at risk, and it is essential for cybersecurity experts to familiarize themselves with quantum cryptography techniques. These new methodologies promise to enhance security through principles like quantum key distribution (QKD), which ensures secure communication channels that cannot be easily intercepted without detection. By understanding and engaging with these advancements, security professionals can not only protect their organizations but also contribute to the broader dialogue on effective quantum-safe practices.

Proactive measures are imperative as we embrace the quantum future. Cybersecurity professionals must take steps to prepare their infrastructures for the inevitable changes that quantum computing will bring to the threat landscape. This includes assessing current cybersecurity frameworks for vulnerabilities that quantum algorithms could exploit. Investing in ongoing education and training on quantum cryptography will equip professionals with the knowledge needed to implement appropriate countermeasures. Collaborating with researchers and participating in forums or communities dedicated to quantum security will also help in staying ahead of potential threats. Organizations should consider transitioning to post-quantum cryptographic standards proactively, ensuring that their encryption methods remain robust against quantum attacks, ultimately securing sensitive data more effectively.

Recognizing the evolving nature of threats is vital in developing resilient strategies. Staying informed about the latest research in quantum cryptography not only fortifies individual expertise but also arms the entire security team with cutting-edge knowledge. Regularly testing and updating security protocols in light of new quantum developments should be a standard practice. By fostering a culture of curiosity and vigilance within the cybersecurity community, professionals can adapt to the challenges posed by quantum advancements. Emphasizing this adaptive mindset will be key to navigating the future landscape of cybersecurity effectively.